comfortable
COUNTRY

comfortable
COUNTRY

ENRICA STABILE

photography by Christopher Drake
text by Julia Watson

RYLAND
PETERS
& SMALL
LONDON NEW YORK

First published in Great Britain in 2001
by Ryland Peters & Small
20–21 Jockey's Fields
London WC1R 4BW
This compact edition published 2005

10 9 8 7 6 5 4 3 2

ISBN: 1 84172 868 3

Printed in China

For this edition
Designer Luana Gobbo
Senior Editor Clare Double
Location and Picture Research Emily Westlake
Production Jacquie Horner
Art Director Gabriella Le Grazie
Publishing Director Alison Starling

European Locations Enrica Stabile

www.rylandpeters.com

CONTENTS

an introduction to comfortable country

To me, comfort is almost synonymous with country. I don't mean the comfort of a large, air-conditioned home. To be at ease, you need something different. Country is not simply an area you can find on a map, it is a place of the spirit. Even the simplest home in the country can be like heaven. Comfortable country style is not just about owning a house on a hill, on the edge of a wood in the mountains, on a cliff or on a sandy beach at the seaside. It is about a different way of living, more simply and peacefully, as time passes.

I would like to share my recipe for well-being. Leave town, go to a place you love and that is important to you, and look carefully around you at the smallest details: a blade of grass, a ladybird on the windowsill, or a ray of sunlight coming through the windows, lighting thousands of tiny dust particles. Sit outside and refresh your mind with this wonderful place. Unlike in a town apartment, the view constantly changes according to the light, the season and the time of day.

If you do not own a country retreat, think about nature in your urban home. Slow to a quieter rhythm, focus on the changing seasons, and try to create an inviting and peaceful atmosphere. Use simple materials to make your interiors naturally elegant, with a combination of beautiful utilitarian objects and treasured country-style antiques. Your home will welcome you with warmth and friendliness and an atmosphere of complete well-being.

OPPOSITE TOP LEFT
This corner epitomizes comfortable country style: a calm, peaceful atmosphere created by beautiful pale paint and touches of natural wicker, cloth and wool. The painted cupboard houses bedroom linen, while the garden chair is an informal touch.

OPPOSITE TOP RIGHT
The purity of this simple yet romantic bedroom, with its tied muslin curtain at the window, is warmed by a checked blanket.

OPPOSITE BOTTOM LEFT Light streams through the windows of this sitting room, which houses an amazing collection including animal horns and monumental busts and urns.

OPPOSITE BOTTOM RIGHT A warm yellow entrance hall is complemented by the duck-egg blue front door. Flowers stand ready to greet visitors, while a colourful rag runner leads towards the oak staircase.

COUNTRY
INFLUENCES

CHANGING SEASONS

LEFT Any time of year, flowers make a decorative point. In this light-filled corner, a galvanized bucket filled with an informal bunch of blue catmint picks up the colour of a painted dresser and storage box.

OPPOSITE LEFT Two folding chairs, set beside a glorious herbaceous border, offer a nonchalant invitation to sit and admire the flowers.

OPPOSITE ABOVE RIGHT Don't be limited to conventional containers. In establishing a sense of ease, this plain mug makes a far more effective holder for a blowsy rose than a glass or china vase.

No one can ignore the seasons. Consciously or not, we have a physical response to them as they alter. In winter, our bodies incline towards hibernation: sweaters and blazing fires are as comforting to the spirit as to the flesh. In the heat of summer, we abandon dark clothing and adopt a more languorous existence. We turn to nature's palette below the horizon for the colours of our winter surroundings – earth, the trunks of trees, stones and berries. In summer, our minds wander to the sun, the sea and the clearer, lighter shades of natural warmth.

Changes in the seasons can be reflected in our rooms without upheaval. The mood is established in the details. Herald the informality of early spring with a simple glass jar of hedgerow flowers, or summer with a colourful bunch of blooms from your garden border. In the warmer seasons, take up the rugs from your floors. Remove clutter. Leave behind only those pieces you absolutely love. Clear

open windows and doors
to admit the springtime

crisp white touches
are the essence of
summer

away the ashes from an open fireplace and stow cushions, rugs and eiderdowns – cosy barricades against the bitter chill – away in cupboards, trunks and boxes until the year turns again. In this way rooms are unburdened and given a chance to breathe with greater lightness, in tune with the breezes that waft freely through opened windows. The pale blues of warmer skies and pinks and yellows of spring buds echo the colours in nature. Brought inside, they reflect our desire for a fresh start. As temperatures climb and days lengthen, our optimism and sense of openness are renewed.

White, the purest of hues, hums with a clarity against which all the other shades of summer will sing. Summer is the time of year for crisp white sheets, tablecloths embroidered with flowers, cushions in

OPPOSITE AND ABOVE A wide covered porch makes a perfect summer bedroom with outdoor shower. Lengths of white fabric draped over the bed's canopy, a breezy sail of white sheet to provide the shower's essential privacy and a basket of towels all celebrate languid days of comfortable living.

LEFT Placing the vibrant reds of summer fruits and vegetables in front of a window box of fresh contrasting green brings the glow of the season indoors. The diversity of the elements on the table gives the display its informality.

a jug of rushes, twigs and bright berries
sounds a perfect autumn note

faded floral cottons or candy-pink stripes on white. White is imperative. Cover sofas and chairs upholstered in winter colours with damask tablecloths, yards of muslin or calico. Their folds and pleats as you tuck them in conveys informality and ease. With white as a clean background, touches of colour can be added without obscuring the freshness. But keep the colours and details simple. For the best summery effect, stick to one colour plus white in each room. In a blue and white room, line a pretty collection of blue spongeware on top of a chest of drawers. In a white and pink one, use cushions trimmed in pink or covered in fabric of pink blossoms. Old glass scent bottles make an appealing display upon a side table. Create displays you can change with the seasons: in winter, place pine cones, candlesticks and coloured glassware along a mantel; in summer,

BELOW LEFT Richly coloured Provençal dishes deserve to be shown off.

BELOW RIGHT Bronze urns and architectural ornaments surround a Louis XVI chest of drawers. The display depends on strong shapes and monotones.

OPPOSITE Flowers in a shining copper vat echo those painted on the doors of the 1730s Bavarian armoire in the dining room.

THIS PAGE One key to the comfortable country look is a feeling of spontaneity in the arrangement of objects, but remember the fine line between an unforced display and untidiness. This front hall contains a number of different articles, but each has a point – in the appeal of its shape, as with the garden urns, or its usefulness to the household.

arrange a collection of seashells, driftwood and stones. It's spring cleaning with the eye.

In autumn and winter rooms, more than one colour can be used in happy conjunction, but keep them within the same spectrum of nature; the golds, dark greens and rich blushes of turning leaves or the greys, taupes, darker browns and colder blues of deeper winter. Ambers, plums, forest greens and sapphires also belong to autumn and winter.

As the weather turns cold, pile rugs back onto the floor, fold thickly woven blankets over the arms of sofas and chairs and place a log basket or pile of kindling near the fire. Cast intimate pools of light with a variety of table lamps, instead of depending upon a striking central light source. Draw curtains against the cold and dark and enjoy nurturing food.

These are responses to nature we can echo with ease in our surroundings. A ceramic jug of rushes and twigs beaded with bright berries sounds the perfect autumn note. A voluptuous throw of nubbled weaves in jewelled colours or plaids, laid across a bed or sofa, creates the perfect mood in winter. Then add piles of rich cushions and mounds of comforting blankets and any whisper of the bitter chill outside is banished. Whatever nature is doing outside, you can reflect it – or protect yourself against it – in your safe haven indoors.

TOP The French cane day bed, generous cushion and throw are a call to settle down with a book. Behind, on the table, is a collage of seaweeds.

ABOVE A workbasket filled with sewing and knitting materials suggests time for hobbies and peaceful domestic activities.

PEACEFULNESS

In today's fast-moving world, home should be a haven of renewal; it needn't be a showcase for trends. Comfortable country style reminds us that some things are timeless. A monogrammed pillowcase brings to mind a less urgent period; flowers on a windowsill encourage us to enjoy the simple beauty around us. It's an uncomplicated look. This doesn't mean it casts elegance or style aside: it is as distinctive as anything at the cutting edge of design, but far easier to live with.

Comfortable country conveys a sense of peace and harmony. Its clarity and simplicity transmit, in a contemporary setting, a seductive peacefulness that contrasts with blowsy chintzes and tassels.

OPPOSITE In this almost monastically uncluttered bedroom, the understated look is established by the carved green frieze above the bed and the green silk cover upon it. Crisp white linen on plump pillows and piles of woollen sweaters, blankets or throws left tidily exposed on shelves convey a message of comfort and security while looking alluring.

THIS PAGE To generate a sense of peace in any room, keep each of its elements clear. Restrict the colour palette, control clutter, allow the space to breathe. In this French bedroom, the only pattern to break the white theme is the delicate print on the quilt. This allows the distinctive line of the crapaud (toad) armchair's iron frame to make an impact.

It is as classic as a brocades-and-silk style, but aims to enfold us in serenity and ease.

Clarity is the guide. Each household item and piece of furniture should count as useful or comfortable. With this idea at its heart, home becomes a placid retreat, created from simple elements. Restrict colour schemes to one or two per room, and limit patterns to cushions or throws.

Gingham, stripes, ticking, or faded florals on tea-stained backgrounds are all redolent of old-fashioned charm and imbue a room with a sense of peace. They can provide a perfect foil for a diverse range of furniture from any period, toning down hard edges. Use these traditional materials with equal effect at windows, on chairs and sofas and to cover cushions.

an uncomplicated scene
set apart from a busy life
is a retreat

OPPOSITE Green is one of the most restful colours to live with. A breezy shade of spearmint paint is applied to the porch floor of this elegant Long Island retreat, as well as to the swing. By uniting the two with colour, decorative diversions, like the mix of cushion covers, don't jar the eye.

THIS PAGE This white marbled-topped iron garden table adds an unceremonious note to a country sitting room where white is a key colour. A reminder of its outdoor origins is given by the white-painted metal basket containing a rich display of roses. Behind is a painted rose trellis.

An eclectic collection of pottery jugs on a side table, simple green and white crockery or a row of pegs hung with shawls and scarves all offer calmness and serenity. We sense their message of domestic peace. They evoke a time when decoration was not designed to dramatize or excite; it existed as a restorative background to daily life. Simple displays, emphasizing the activities of the household, are as effective today in city or country settings. Try an armoire stacked with an assortment of crockery (in the same or toning colours or it will simply look untidy). With linens, you can heap several piles of different colours, as long as each pile is the same colour throughout – or again you will merely create a mess. Sets of linens tied with ribbons like birthday presents convey a country charm.

If you have high ceilings, remember the tops of cupboards and armoires, where you can show off an orderly stack of pretty blankets, a collection of hatboxes or old leather suitcases. Exposing these personal objects creates a mood of comfort.

Even formal set pieces can convey simplicity, if the components accord – the placing of a glass ornament or vase upon a white-painted desk or side table, perhaps under a

THIS PAGE To bring brilliance into a room, arrange attractive pieces of glass on tabletops where they can reflect, and sparkle in, the source of light. Junk-shop finds of glass scent bottles, jugs and bowls make a pretty display. Decanters can take on a new role accentuating light coming in from a sunny window.

THIS PAGE Natural light is a decorative element that lifts the spirits. Take advantage of it. To suggest space, emphasize or frame incoming light with white or pale paint. Or place a chair where light floods in, to draw attention to its presence and make the most of it in comfort.

THIS PAGE The feeling of calm in this upstairs corridor comes from the light pouring in from two large skylights. The temptation to fill the space with tables and other furniture often found in halls has been resisted. Only a slatted chair, wall sconces and modest decorations interrupt this spacious passage.

mercuried mirror, each article mimicking the essence of the other. This is at the heart of Gustavian style, so much part of the serenity of Swedish country houses. It captures a soothing stillness in pared-down details, pale painted furniture, and walls and floors all washed in the same continuous colour. All these elements are part of comfortable country style today.

Old-fashioned paint finishes such as distemper, flat oil paint or casein milk paint, often tinted with the soft hues of natural pigments, can be used to good effect. Distemper, which gives a pleasantly chalky finish, was once popular for covering poor plaster walls yet flatters today's smoother surfaces. Flat oil paint offers a very matt finish and looks good on woodwork, but marks easily. Oil eggshell is a practical alternative to this as it marks less, but it does have a slight sheen. These washes and paints, along with natural pigments, are available from discerning paint suppliers and mixers.

Accessibility is the basis of comfortable country appeal. A glut of pattern and texture is visually indigestible, discouraging a sense of ease, and its opposite, minimalism, demands that the things we like to have about us – books, a piece of sewing – should be tidied away in order not to disturb the clean lines of the style. The intrinsic peacefulness in comfortable country includes accepting the restful ebb and flow of life.

ABOVE With great aplomb, this sitting room window has been hung with printed voile curtains in two colours that echo the freshness of the garden beyond. Floating airily inside a formal draped pelmet, they add a touch of frivolity to an otherwise serious piece of decoration.

NOSTALGIA

ABOVE A prettily monogrammed pillow is highlighted upon an old rush-seated chair – classic white on white.

RIGHT Childhood treasures or pretty items collected at antique fairs fit happily into comfortable country style. Give pride of place to an old wooden plaything that is as attractive in its craftsmanship as in the sentiment it evokes.

OPPOSITE The country flowers of Victorian storybooks make for a gently nostalgic mood. Whether part of the embroidered design on a tablecloth, or plunged into a rustic jug, flowers strike an essential chord. Florals look good contrasted with stripes.

Somewhere in everyone's imagination is a place where easygoing afternoons ended with golden cakes and jams full of fruit, and where sprigged eiderdowns and faded quilts bulged on beds in lavender-scented rooms. Where time ran more slowly and summers were always warm, the sweet smell of new-mown lawns filled the air, and bees buzzed in flowerbeds.

This image recalls a time when routines seemed fixed from one year to the next, from seaside sand in the sandwiches to hand-knitted scarves wound around winter necks. A conkers-on-string time, with drifts of dry leaves to kick, and hot chocolate to come home to; a bugs-in-jam-jars time, with daisy chains to weave.

The gleam of polished wood, the scent of vanilla, the crunch of frost underfoot: even now these sights, smells and sounds evoke an age when there was always time to crumble lavender into a bowl, to stare at logs crackling in the grate, to gather baskets of berries and pick flowers. Time too to hang out linen to catch

gusts of air among its folds, and store it carefully, with oranges stuck with cloves or pomanders between the sheets.

Memory is a capricious faculty. The sight of an old luggage label or faded bundle of ribbons can remind us of a period that might not even have been our own. Such thoughts don't need to come from personal experience. What matters is the way we can respond to them. Nostalgia is no less poignant for being a brief encounter with someone else's past. Its flavour is worth recapturing for the sense of comfort and simplicity it brings.

In these times of mass manufacture, we miss the intimacy of the past, the sense of contact with something personal that is conveyed by a piece of handworked lace or the embroidered edge of a rough cotton cloth. Details like these map out the hours some unknown hand worked diligently at their design. You can recreate similar images quite simply. Make a start by scenting your linen cupboards with lavender bags or bars of gloriously fragranced soap. Even hand towels piled on a simple kitchen chair suggest a leisurely and more comfortable existence.

We have become too quick to throw away and replace. Before you abandon that basket whose willow may have unravelled around the rim, or throw out that finished jar of preserves, consider if it offers the possibility of another role. Set by the front door, the basket might be just the place for gloves that

OPPOSITE The witty metal-work chandelier adds a frivolous touch to a restful kitchen. The leisurely mood is conveyed by the idiosyncratic collection of pottery jugs along the shelf and the wall sconces above the kitchen counter.

BELOW LEFT Old French enamel containers are suitably nostalgic, while a frieze of patterned or laced paper, or embroidered fabric, pinned along the shelf, borrows effectively from the past.

BELOW RIGHT Store ingredients on open shelves in containers like these in pottery and tin, more pleasing than standard glass jars. The jugs above are not just for display.

THIS PAGE Bold fabric adds a romantic flourish above a painted French Directoire bed. The rag rug has been picked for its soft shades that echo the American quilt.

separate themselves in drawers, house keys and other essentials that jumble up in entrance halls. A row of jam jars along a bathroom windowsill or shelf could carry toothbrushes, tubes of paste or coloured ends of soap. Suddenly these things cease to be irritants you can't wait to discard, and take on an interest of their own.

A country look with a touch of nostalgia is easy to create. Simplicity is the key. Use pale paint and washes on walls; wallpaper suggests formal receiving rooms. Give table lamps shades of plain or painted parchment, or a gathering of simply patterned fabric. Add rugs of hook-worked pieces from the scrap bag – an informal mix of colours, patterns and textures. Mats of heavy wools, pulled in patterns through sackcloth backing, or rag rugs in coloured stripes of rough ripped cloth, are cottage coverings still easy to find. Curtains found in junk shops and jumble sales, faded at the edges; a pile of sweaters in soft earthy shades on a wooden stool; an old basketweave chair half-draped with a blanket: uncomplicated things such as these convey the comfort and ease of simple country style. In fact, it takes little more than a faded quilt tossed over a modern sofa, a collection of pottery and china vases along a shelf, or a display of woven baskets, old fabric-covered boxes or *objets trouvés* that come with a history of long and fond usage to cast a country mood over a modern urban living room.

TOP A pile of antique boxes, covered in faded fabric prints and redolent of history, brings a sentimental link with the past to a bedside table.

ABOVE The beautifully monogrammed towel and the pretty china bowl of soaps it is resting beneath connect to an age when spare time was usefully spent with needle and thread.

recapture the unassuming
style of a contented era
not so long ago

It's a style entirely open to personal interpretation and so can work happily with contemporary pieces. A mellow leather hatbox is for one person a place to store outdoor shoes, for another a useful place to keep bedside books. An old pie safe is just the thing for bathroom lotions, or tea cloths and napkins in a kitchen corner. Country style reflects a time before mass production, before factory outpourings of identical items made uniqueness scarce. It's a personal affair, an individual reaction to individual things.

Take nature as your cue for colours and materials. The style is modest. Silks, frills and furbelows are best left for a grander stage. Comfortable country homes are content with cotton and wool, gentle ruffles and ribbon. The everyday country kitchenware of past generations was rarely decorated. In France, Italy and Spain, local pottery plates and dishes, often with fluted or scalloped edges, were fired in deep hues of amber, green, blue and terracotta. In England and in the United

OPPOSITE A girl's room is filled with romantic objects and designs inspired by the past. Yet the look is fresh, not gloomy, achieved by emphasizing its delicate lines with lots of white on fabrics and furniture.

ABOVE RIGHT Old silver-topped glass scent bottles add a pretty touch to a plain side table.

BELOW RIGHT Cushions on the bed are a feminine mix of ruffles and lace.

States, paler colours were in common use but shapes were still simple. Even more formal dining china and faience was only modestly decorated, by hand or transfer, with floral patterns or country landscapes in muted blues, browns or burgundies.

Fabric makes a statement. All manner of sources can be explored to find interesting cloth that adds focus to rooms and the pieces of furniture within them. Just one length of old textile can successfully establish the whole look.

Embroidering, appliquéing and quilting have been part of domestic life across continents for centuries. In the United States especially, quilts tell stories and, through their patterning, can reveal exactly where they were made. Such treasures can still be unearthed in attics and antique shops. Pieces like these are generally affordable, and are deeply rewarding to use. The printed colour of an old quilt will have been muted to faded shades of pink, lavender and fern green.

When technology became a fact of life we had to assimilate, many of us turned to minimalism and a pared-down style to reflect the proficiency of our new world. But real people are not suited to behaving as though daily life were a laboratory experiment – cool, clean and clinical. Efficiency has its place, but in the things that we choose to live with we need an intimacy and a softness to keep us gentle, and to keep us human.

OPPOSITE Old French farmhouse armoires were popular in rustic rooms for displaying special china. Here, pretty blue-painted pottery is casually stacked. It is an appealing look easily emulated with modern cupboards; remove centre panels from the doors and replace with chicken wire.

ABOVE The pieces in the collection do not all come from the same set, which adds to the charm of the display. But they are all the same shade of blue, which keeps the group from looking messy. It is important to preserve the unstudied look – its informality is why the display works.

UTILITY

The practical essentials of life need not be unattractive simply because they are useful. There can be such pleasure in the sight of a pile of linen, or a cluster of utensils in a jug. In traditional country homes, the business of running a household was visible. This didn't mean there was no room for charm and making things look their best. The appeal of comfortable country style is that it makes artful use of simple effects to create an unpretentious, relaxing look. Unassuming things – an antique pine washstand with a pretty china water jug, or embroidered cotton towels in the bathroom – inspire a sense of comfort we instantly respond to.

The details to borrow are modest. Cupboard and kitchen shelves might be lined with wallpaper or edged in a paper frieze; patterned tiles used as a splashback

ABOVE A wide, shallow, china-clay farmhouse sink is the perfect scullery basin for cutting and soaking flowers, cleaning leafy vegetables and other household chores. Once collectors' items, they are now common currency at most kitchen suppliers. Exposed pipes add to the rustic charm of this informal room.

RIGHT An old-fashioned egg safe in a cool larder, set on a marble slab. You can also buy reproduction versions. They must be kept in a cool place.

OPPOSITE TOP RIGHT Old enamelware may be too chipped for its original use, but has a country charm that makes perfect containers for a simple bunch of wild flowers.

ABOVE A collection of sun-faded linens makes a pretty public pile on a kitchen sideboard.

LEFT From the ceramic butler's sink to the galvanized dustbin and dowelling dish drainer on the wall, much has been made of natural materials to establish an unpretentious look in this kitchen corner.

behind sinks, basins and baths. Try colourful French-style faience designs of country scenes, deep blue Delft tiles, or Moorish-influenced Portuguese and Spanish tiles in strong blues, sharp greens with yellow, or varied shades of crimson. In addition, old Victorian tiles are still plentiful, and popular, in Britain and the United States.

Colour-sponged or painted enamelled tins, traditional storage in France, Germany and the United States, and tall round wooden boxes from Russian dacha kitchens, with swirling leaf-like patterns in yellow, green and red, can be found in junk and antique shops.

Copy country housewives of times gone by when there weren't such aids to tidiness as modern knife blocks and utensil racks. Bunch ladles, whisks and spoons together in a jug or crock, within easy reach of the stove or sink. Counter tops are a modern device. With comfortable country style, a scrubbed

THIS PAGE A retro 1950s kitchen unit with ingenious cupboards and roll-top bread safe proves that furniture which functions effectively is never out of fashion. Cream high gloss paint and the refrigerator door clasps are smart details to copy.

OPPOSITE Despite its contemporary hob and oven, this kitchen has a comfortable country look. A haphazard mix of materials and levels – marble beneath the patterned tiles, the sink set higher than the cooking zone, the café curtains hiding the plumbing, and the collection of china on the two rustic shelves – tempers suggestions of modernity.

THIS PAGE This high-ceilinged, light-filled space makes a utility room that is charming enough to take extra guests. A thick blanket covered by a pretty cloth makes the perfect ironing board. Period lights and galvanized buckets help imbue the room with the relaxed feel of a bygone age. Blue highlights dilute the functional look.

pine table can become a work surface that is as practical as it is aesthetically pleasing. Store essential supplies, like plastic bottles of cleaning products, waste bins and old cloths, under a free-standing or butler's sink behind a simple curtain drawn along a wire.

Curtains gathered at top and bottom look pretty behind the glazed fronts of cupboards hiding crockery or household linen in more formal rooms. White curtains in a white-painted cupboard look particularly effective. Heavy curtains hanging over doors that lead outside guard against seeping winter draughts (even if you have central heating) and make a room feel cosy; unlined curtains in muslin or coloured voile create a casual atmosphere in summer, and fend off inquisitive flies and insects.

Cleaning tasks will seem more agreeable if your utility area, even if this is simply a kitchen corner, has a country feel. Hang brushes and brooms on hooks,

ABOVE LEFT Concrete softened with a yellow tint forms the surround for a drop-in stainless-steel sink.

CENTRE LEFT Dinner plates piled on a white dresser create a relaxed look.

BELOW LEFT This well-stocked china cupboard sets a comfortable mood while providing practical storage.

and rags along a rack. Cover the ironing board with a pleasing piece of material and expose it folded against the wall. Bring in galvanized iron and zinc rather than plastic buckets and bins. Replace garish plastic brooms, mops and brushes with wood and bristle ones – just as efficient – and try soft yellow dusters and chunks of olive oil soap.

The informality of a country approach can be reflected in everyday storage: wooden egg safes, old glass biscuit jars or enamelled tins. We may not have grown up with the goods and chattels of bygone eras, but the sight of these common objects is comforting, forestalling a more clinical way of living.

ABOVE This large Shaker box might hold any disparate but untidy essentials, like sewing materials or telephone directories.

LEFT Baskets offer attractive storage, particularly for garden produce which needs an air flow to keep fresh, or in a hallway for scarves and gloves.

OPPOSITE Storage is easy in comfortable country homes: simply pick what looks pretty and relaxed. Here, cutlery lives in pots and jars, and serving dishes are decorative on open shelving.

FAR LEFT An attractive iron coat-and-hat stand makes a beguiling, sculptural piece, and replaces a cupboard.

OPPOSITE The rocking horse draws the eye down a flagstoned corridor, into the heart of this English country house. Visitors passing through are caught up in the mood of easy relaxation created by the family living here.

THIS PAGE The fish kettle above the door, terracotta pots of geraniums, wellington boots and patterned curtains are down to earth. Elements such as these, and the rustic box, make comfortable country style.

ABOVE An old long-spouted galvanized watering can goes well with a collection of terracotta pots, and in a city space it will foster a country mood.

LEFT The informality of this country kitchen is readily translated to a city space. At its heart is the calm exposure of every element of kitchen activity, from creative cooking to the practical washing up.

OPPOSITE ABOVE AND BELOW In keeping with the free and easy open look, the only closed cupboards appear below the work surface. Even the storage containers are made of glass to reveal their contents.

NATURAL MATERIALS

THIS PAGE The items in this display may appear haphazard. But the combination of country objects in natural materials has been carefully chosen to establish the casually comfortable look of this entrance hall. The deliberately symmetrical positioning of the two urns brings order to what otherwise might look chaotic.

Nature's elements, such as wood, stone, rushes and grasses, are familiar decorative materials that strike an instinctive chord. The appeal of wooden boxes, stone objects, baskets and carved bowls is immediate. We want to reach out and touch them. Natural materials make beautiful coverings for floors and furniture; reflecting nature is the aim.

Simple textiles – Aegean stripes, Egyptian cottons, checks – fit this look. Make curtains and covers from unfussy linen scrim, muslin, calico and hessian (wash the material before using, as these fabrics tend to shrink). Patterned cottons with botanical prints and stylized flowers make stunning contrasts with these. Simple sprigs, rosebuds, and small blooms with a cottagey feel are comfortable country florals.

Walls, too, reflect nature's softer palette: apply paint in duck-egg blues,

THIS PAGE Such is the freedom to mix and match in comfortable country style that outdoor furniture can find a place indoors. An elegant day bed can be covered with straw-stuffed cushions in almost crude materials, and, in an adventurous move that pays off, wallpaper is torn back to expose the texture of the plaster beneath.

LEFT Architectural salvage warehouses are inspiring sources for items in natural materials that can make a dramatic impact. The column appears to have been chosen for its fluting, matching that in the leg of the Louis XVI commode beside which it stands, and its age-roughened patina.

BELOW In a room decorated in a saturated colour, limit the disparate objects in a collection to one shade – the same as the walls or

dawn blushes, pale moss greens or the greys and sands of pebbles. Rag rub on the paint or colour wash with several thin coats, for a lightly uneven finish that will reflect the light.

In rooms with these backgrounds of almost chalky tones, place pieces that continue the naturally matt finish. Furniture with a reflective sheen, such as ornately carved mahogany, will not work as effectively in conveying the country feel as unvarnished or traditional painted pieces executed in flat or satin paint. Windsor chairs and wheelbacks have such a familiar link with rural settings that they sit well in comfortable country rooms. Rush or cane chairs are clearly casual. If you find these with sagging seats, furnishings, or one in striking contrast – or the eye won't know where to settle. In rooms of pallid, natural shades, keep them to a similar palette. The result won't be rustic or primitive but will reinforce a sense of peace. Here, a collection of carved stone pieces, fossils and antlers brings timeless elegance to a sophisticated monochrome city setting. Part of what makes this room so striking is that there is no quarter given to the softening effect of material – no curtains, rugs or cushions. Fluidity is only expressed in the sculptural lines of the objects on display.

tighten them by saturating the seats on both sides with water, then letting them dry naturally.

Scandinavian country-style settles and armchairs, with their curving painted wood frames, look perfectly at home when their upholstery is kept simple. Gingham, stripes or a small floral print on a white background are striking. Button-backed nursing chairs convey a relaxed feel when they are covered in a heavy-weave undyed parchment cotton or a tea-stained floral fabric. Large, overstuffed sofas and armchairs in loose covers are far more suggestive of comfortable country than when upholstered in a formal fabric. Recycle old knitwear as patchwork throws, or cushion covers

THIS PAGE The house in these pictures is striking because the decoration sticks to a palette of blues, leaving no doubt as to what the owner's favourite colour is.

OPPOSITE The Gustavian clock in the sitting room is the starting point for a Scandinavian mood contrived through a collection of simple country pieces in blues and pale greys. The unassuming one-drawer chest fits in well with the raw table and informal sofa. These things have a lived-in look that suggests a room where shoes can be kicked off and feet rested on the table, yet it's thoroughly stylish.

fastened with bone or wood buttons: particularly effective when the original sweaters are in natural colours.

Contemporary rugs often have a very uniform pile or a strident pattern. Here is where rag rugs, hook rugs, or the traditional wide woollen weaves of Welsh and New England runners and rugs come into their own. Kelims and oriental rugs are timeless. In sunny rooms, colourful Greek rugs look terrific, particularly as they begin to fade with washing. Sisal and seagrass, patently natural materials, look as good in wall-to-wall covering as they do

OPPOSITE A table and seating formed from stone slabs make the perfect spot on the shaded terrace of a stone house. The use of the flowerpot as shade for a light adds a witty touch in keeping with the use of natural materials in this attractive corner.

LEFT Bricks exposed to view in a window seat offer a rustic touch, tempered by cushions and curtains dressed in simple fabrics. Their warm blues are echoed in the china collection.

BELOW A wooden crate, like this one painted Colonial blue and sitting on an American Windsor chair, makes a clever holder for plant pots.

in an island rug. Hard-wearing, and very effective even in a formal setting, they come in simple or complex weaves, some with colours introduced. Terracotta tiles don't have to be limited to kitchen use. Like stone flags, they make handsome flooring and an elegant background for any rug.

Painting floorboards is a striking, economical way to cover the floor that increases the light and, when using the same colour as on the walls or woodwork, gives an impression of greater size. Add several coats of varnish to prevent the paint from scratching.

Once you have decorated a room, underline the feel with details. Here is where you can have fun. Stone garden urns, spotted with lichen, make a stunning impact on an indoor table or mantel. A pretty Victorian birdcage, set where the light from a window can travel through its delicate bars; seashells along a

LEFT Why not demonstrate an appreciation of wood, the warmest and most generous of natural materials? Here, picturesque, paint-peeling folding chairs are stored propped open in this shelter off the garden, giving the wry impression that this area should be celebrated by people taking the time to sit and admire it. They add a decorative touch that makes a set piece out of a practical storage place.

RIGHT Old beams are too often painted over. Exposed, they add a glow that justifies the effort required to strip them, although sand-blasting is laborious and leaves a film of dust over every surface in the house for a considerable time after the job is finished.

mantel; terracotta flowerpots filled with plants – all carry the theme of pastoral idyll. Newspapers can be tossed into a wooden basket or stencilled crate by an armchair, while glass garden bells and lobster pots can double as shades for hanging lights. Light shining through these graphic shapes is dramatic, but use low-watt bulbs or they will dazzle, and fix fittings securely.

Elements like these remind us of the pleasure we derive from the integrity of natural materials and living with things shaped by human hands from nature's bounty.

COUNTRY
ROOMS

COUNTRY
LIVING ROOMS

A welcoming sofa, a vase of flowers and a few favourite pieces. With simple but well-chosen ingredients you can create a living room that is a place of perfect comfort.

Comfortable country style lends itself to an easeful look. This need not imply that you will veer towards a lack of elegance. Any room that is uncomplicated will be a relaxing one to sit in. Easy on the eye, it shouldn't contain too many elements fighting for attention. Armchairs should look inviting, enticing you to curl up in them with a good book. A side table within reach to support a lamp or a bowl of flowers confirms the feel.

In your living room, begin by considering what you want its focal point to be. It might be the view through a window, a wall on which you hang a favourite painting or a fireplace. Next, decide seating and where you plan to place it. Your most important furniture decision will be the sofa. You may choose not to have one – groups of cosy armchairs look very congenial. Two sofas can be set with a low table between them, or placed in an L-shape. Big sofas with a sociable saggy appearance, in loose, untailored linen covers, piled with throws and cushions to sink into, are seductive. However, a sofa that's a little more structured is just as appropriate when the informality is conveyed by its upholstery – a wide stripe in funfair candy

your living room is a reflection
of your private self — to truly relax
and be comfortable here, you have
to be yourself

THIS PAGE AND OPPOSITE This modest country house brims with its owner's personality. Distinctly feminine, it has been decorated with an unexpected sumptuousness that never becomes too fussy. Extravagantly sized cushions slump over the stone staircase leading down from the hall and along the built-in seating beside the fire; tables are covered with thick capacious cloths; and swathes of lightweight materials are draped dramatically around the windows. Yet by keeping white as the predominant colour, none of this opulence is too much and an easy elegance prevails in this fundamentally plain cottage.

THIS PAGE AND OPPOSITE ABOVE White establishes a totally relaxing mood. This room is modest in size, with tiled stairs in one corner leading upstairs. By adhering to white in its decoration and keeping it uncluttered, the space feels generous and restful. Furniture and ornaments are simple. Even the floor is rug free, increasing the feeling of space.

BELOW Again, white forms the background to a room that is invitingly comfortable. The armchair looks cosy thanks to its gathered skirt, while the use of colour on its cushions and on the covers of those cushions in the alcove lounging area draws the eye to them and encourages an awareness that these are places in which to relax thoroughly.

pink, or bold blue and white checks. These aren't earnest fabrics. They sing with a country freshness. Or take a sofa with graphic lines. Lay a length of cloth along the seat or across the back, and immediately you deflate its solemnity. Even the formality of a more decorative Gustavian sofa can be tempered by pale painted walls and furniture to imbue the living room with tranquillity.

Any sitting room is rendered simple by keeping every major piece in it in one colour. This can be very effective when that colour is white. Splashes of a different shade can be added in cushions,

THIS PAGE Informal seating creates a relaxing atmosphere. This window seat is inviting and intimate, with feminine colours and lace at the window.

OPPOSITE The built-in sofa in this barn-like summer poolhouse is a tranquil spot offering comfort among its generous abundance of cushions.

sofa throws, rugs or bowls of flowers. Colour is crucial in setting the tone. For example, in a confidently elegant living room containing treasures in elemental wood, stone, bone and glass, keep the background to a single colour – say a spectrum of whites. At the other end of the scale, jewel colours like sapphire, amethyst or emerald inspire contentment, by bringing in the vibrant tones we associate with warmth and sunshine.

Classic patterns and materials, used in an unconventional manner, shy away from formality. In a room decorated in a striking toile de Jouy, using the upholstery design on the walls makes for a far from conservative outcome. A sofa in front of a large window may have a traditionally tailored cover. But placing a patio-style wooden chair and a garden bench in front of it, and having florals as the sofa material to echo the greenery outside, makes the setting relaxed.

Keep window treatments simple. Unadorned poles with gathered curtains made up in plain or uncomplicated

OPPOSITE Windows are wonderful places to sit by. This sumptuous sofa oozes comfort and calls out for someone to relax among the cushions. The mix of prints, which reflects the garden beyond the unusual single pane, is soothing because it is kept to soft tones.

RIGHT Here too, the variety of different patterns and materials used for the cushions has an inviting appeal.

materials and patterns work best. Unwelcome views can be disguised with plain muslin or voile.

How you introduce light is important. Candelabras and chandeliers have wonderful flowing lines. But err on the side of restraint in design. Anything too ornate will look out of place. Candles can be put to use on mantels or in clusters in the fireplace. Mirrors double any light and enlarge space. Old ones in unpainted pine frames or French faux bamboo, their backs a little bitten, have immense charm.

Table lamps with gingham, floral or American Colonial-style cut-parchment-work shades make a comfortable country statement. The pools of light from lamps are far more intimate and informal than the fiercer glare from one central fixture.

ABOVE LEFT Not only does the striking antique mirror increase light and the sense of space, but it makes a decorative statement. The patterned candlesticks on the white Gustavian desk add an appealing sculptural interest and draw attention to the mirror above.

OPPOSITE RIGHT
Deliberately chosen details
will add focus to a room.
Individual flowers in glass
bottles make a charmingly
casual display that softens
an imposing formal
mantelpiece. It's an idea
that puts a collection of
pretty scent bottles and
decanters to effective use.

LEFT Draping a throw and
assorted cushions over the
elegant sofa in a period
city house relaxes its
modern lines. Informality
is introduced to this urban
setting through country
pieces, united by a white
paint finish.

BELOW On the pretty
Gustavian settle, a
rectangular cushion points
out its appealing shape.

fresh flowers bring a room to life:
handpicked blooms in
a collection of favourite glass
bottles and vases
look effortless

BELOW LEFT A scalloped border makes the cover of this armchair as unceremonious as a summer skirt. The shape of this original touch is echoed in the glass chandelier used as table decoration. So close to the window, its cut-glass pendants trap the sunlight.

BELOW RIGHT The white china cupboard is positioned where it will absorb and reflect the light coming in from outside.

OPPOSITE This informal, light-filled sitting room has a nostalgic feel. Folds of fine voile at the windows, a sofa throw of lace, the crochet-worked mat beneath the bowl of roses, and a wicker veranda chair are all suggestive of a tea party attended by women in veiled hats – and all contribute to the atmosphere. The old-fashioned bed tray has been given a new lease of life, serving as a witty coffee table.

Country farmhouse finds, like lidded enamelled churns, thick glass cider jars or pottery crocks, can be converted into appealing lamp bases. Ceramic or wooden bases in simple cylindrical or rectangular shapes are effective. Wall sconces made from metal, or even plaster or tile meant for a garden, have a guileless feel.

Fresh flowers bring a room to life. Anything home grown will encourage a comfortable country feel: mixed flowers in a pretty jug, or large terracotta pots of daisies set on the floor, look effortlessly relaxed. Old-fashioned roses strike a timeless note. During autumn and winter, display bowls of dried lavender or rose-petal pot pourri to add a seasonal touch and scent. A basket of pine cones ready to throw on the fire has the same effect.

candlesticks in cut
glass or silver set on side
tables close to a window
reflect daylight

COUNTRY KITCHENS

A pot of basil set near the stove, ivory china on a cream-painted dresser – comfort and tranquillity in the kitchen and dining room are conveyed by simple touches like these.

Cooking and eating can be relaxing occupations, and should be enjoyed in comfortable surroundings. Culinary fashion no longer requires sauces to be reduced to within a splash of their lives; this also takes the pressure off the way our kitchens and dining rooms look. Where and how you cook and eat depends primarily on how much space you have. If your dining room is separate from your kitchen, consider it as another living room. Do you want space for sitting away from the table before or after the meal, on a sofa or in a window seat? Is there a working fireplace in the room and enough space for a table in front of it that the backs of diners won't burn? And what sort of table do you plan to install? A table designed specifically for a dining room is likely to be more formal than the average kitchen table. Your choice of table is especially key if you expect to eat in the kitchen. Here, the table you eat off is likely to do double duty as a work surface. A scrubbed pine table or a plank tabletop on a pair of trestles sets an immediately accommodating tone.

If you then install free-standing pieces of furniture instead of built-in systems, you create an even more informal setting. Shelved cupboards and armoires for crockery and glass are good-looking repositories with a country feel; chests of drawers make just as efficient storage for pots and pans as do kitchen units. It may

ABOVE A 'dresser' has been created out of wall shelves hung above a wood-topped sideboard. While it provides storage for the household's dinnerware, its practicality has not been allowed to override its visual appeal. The display of plates is carefully ordered and arranged.

THIS PAGE Honeyed wood on cupboard doors, table and chairs makes a kitchen-dining room congenially informal. Kitchen equipment, herbs and utensils are hung on hooks in a decorative touch that effectively reinforces the relaxed spirit of the room.

THIS PAGE Some things strike an immediate chord of comfort and serenity: a generous kitchen range, a cosy blanket loosely covering a chair, and the tools for food preparation and eating happily on display.

a farmhouse range draws people to its warm generosity in country or city

be that a galley arrangement is the most practical in your space. In this case, think about installing a prefabricated counter unit carcass, but hanging your own pine doors or pretty curtains. The same approach works with shelving built from brick or wood.

Pots and pans can be brought out on show, with oven cloths and herbs, hung from hooks or rails within easy reach of the stove. Having the necessary tools and equipment to hand makes cooking as relaxing to perform as to watch. Spoons, spatulas and slices can be plunged into an old jug; lids and chopping boards kept in wire baskets; potted herbs ranged along a windowsill. If it looks casual, everyone will feel casual.

THIS PAGE The kitchen is one public room that people are seldom dismayed to find in a state of industrious disarray. Cupboards and shelves filled with crockery, ingredients or carefully arranged pretty bowls make a beguiling sight, like these displays of charming period china and packaging.

The stove, too, is a serious issue. A large farmhouse range establishes a sense of comfort and ease, drawing people and pets to hang around its ample generosity. But a similar response can be inspired by a more casual cooking arrangement: a below-counter wall oven with hob above, set into a tiled surround, for example. A sense of informality is best conveyed by keeping larger appliances below counter level, rather than the more conventional urban look of double ovens installed at shoulder height. A free-standing refrigerator is more likely to give a city kitchen a comfortable country feel than a built-in appliance.

Sinks can also set the tone. Large china clay butler's sinks are generally deeper than off-the-peg stainless-steel sinks and consequently far more practical. French farmhouse sinks, also ceramic, are shallow but usually much wider. The extra space of both makes washing leafy vegetables or handling fish easier. Companies selling

LEFT AND OPPOSITE Here a dining area with its own atmosphere has been created within a large country kitchen. A 1930s-style table provides generous dining space beneath an elaborate chandelier and is surrounded by ochre garden chairs. This dining zone is demarcated by the old Spanish rug upon which the table sits, and the presence of a wicker chaise longue and armchair by the French doors in which to relax. Equally, the cooking area is defined by a breakfast table set at an angle, parallel to the range, under a billiard light that points up the different use of this area.

take a length of
gingham or a floral
sheet as tablecloth, or large
napkins to suggest a

generous
host

professional catering equipment can put you in touch with manufacturers who will design stainless-steel sinks to any depth or width you desire, with integrated, seamless draining boards and preparation areas on either side that are a boon to the serious cook. Lined up next to a wooden surfaced or marble-topped table or drawered chest, their industrial appearance is toned down. You can also have sinks and work surfaces made out of concrete in a natural or a stained colour (be careful not to put glass or china down too quickly, or it will shatter). You may need to reinforce any floor that is not at ground level, to take the extra weight.

Old brass taps look wonderfully rustic, but make sure that junk-shop basket finds have a thread compatible with your plumbing system. Taps bought in France, for instance, often won't fit in Britain or the United States. Hospital taps, with their long handles running parallel to the back of the sink, are immensely practical for turning on and off with elbows when you are busy making pastry. Should you prefer not to have a splashback – though marble, stone, and plain or patterned tiles all promote a comfortable country look – make sure you paint the wall behind the sink or stove with an acrylic or a gloss paint so that you can wipe the wall down and keep it from staining.

Before you decide on lighting, consider how and where you work. Lighting should be placed so that you do not cast a shadow over your preparation area. Similarly, will you want to shed several pools of light over your dining table, or just one, or will the place where you eat be illuminated from the walls with the table softly candlelit? You don't want

ABOVE AND OPPOSITE Here a dining table is tucked into the cosy corner of an entrance hall. The built-in seating area beside the imposing fireplace, with its piles of over-sized cushions, sets a carefree tone of luxury and relaxation that is accentuated by the looped voile pelmet. Using printed fabric for the cushions and tablecloth keeps the look casual and comfortable.

OPPOSITE This dining room mixes different patterns, but in similar hues. The checks on the covers of the folding garden chairs echo the green of the curtains behind the glass cupboard doors. The quilted tablecloth borrows from a classic Victorian fashion.

THIS PAGE Shades of blue play a strong role in the decoration of this kitchen, with blue patterned wallpaper, the pretty dresser door frames highlighted in a strong shade, and a blue and white frieze lining the shelves. Blue continues in the tiles and jugs around the marble sink.

anything so modern that it looks out of place, but you do want it to be effective. Opaque glass shades look immensely appealing on hanging lamps and, along with enamelled or metal saucer-shaped shades, can still be picked up at antique fairs or in junk shops.

If you are planning on a single kitchen-dining room and it is a room large enough to keep the two elements well apart, you can visually separate the dining area by running the lighting on a two-circuit system so that both ends of the room are not necessarily lit at once. A dimmer on the dining-end circuit is also a good idea. If it is a small room with space for only a little table, try turning it into a stylish kitchen-dining room with a very French, almost boudoir feel. Hang a pretty but unexpected glass chandelier above a curvaceous set of iron café chairs and table, and paint the room in pale pastel colours.

Different lamps or lampshades establish the two separate areas further, as will a change in flooring. You might, at the working end of the room, have an easy-to-clean tiled or stone floor and, at the dining end, wooden floorboards, parquet or a large rug. In a city kitchen that is not at ground level, be sure to find out how much weight the ceiling of the room below can take before you go ahead with stone flooring.

Once you have organized the main pieces, bring in accessories that will confirm the look. In the kitchen, classic ironware, enamelware and terracotta cooking equipment is as handsome and efficient today as it ever was. Similarly, pottery, glassware and china can be as casual and diverse as you please. Almost any pottery – plain, patterned or coloured – can be set out successfully alongside wooden bowls, metal chargers and bone

bring the country
inside: abundant pots
of greenery suggest
a conservatory
dining room

LEFT A pleasing country-style cushion for this Windsor chair has been sewn out of cotton tea cloths.

FAR LEFT The imposing cast-iron fireplace, with its display of handsome pewter chargers along the mantelshelf, draws the eye in this simple but comfortable dining room. Its austere lines are softened by the pottery display. Any style of furniture other than the absolutely plain pine table and kitchen chairs would risk seeming excessive against it. Restraint continues in the style of the simple lampshade, and the curtains hung on a plain metal pole.

spoons. One-off handmade pieces have a particular charm, but simple mass-produced shapes in sunshine colours, like the Fiestaware of 1950s America, also have a wonderful appeal. Patterned dinner services in soft berry or moss colours on an ivory background still convey a comfortable country feel without being quite so rudimentary in style. Plain cream china on a plain cream-painted dresser looks as effective in a kitchen or dining room as a glaze-fronted cupboard filled with a disparate collection of pretty pieces of pottery in blues. Equally, laying a table with mismatched plates and bistro-style tumblers can be as warmly welcoming as the more formal array of a Provençal dinner service on a scrubbed pine table. In the absence of old embroidered napkins, use plain or patterned tea cloths; their exuberant size suggests a liberal host.

COUNTRY
BEDROOMS

One room in which you must be able to
relax is the bedroom. The easy, serene style
of a comfortable country bedroom makes
the perfect place for refreshing rest.

RIGHT Quilts, bed linen and pillows of different patterned blues are layered, giving this bedroom, with its painted iron bedsteads and fantasy muslin canopies hanging from a painted frieze, a peaceful aspect.

BELOW An appliquéd cushion adds a personal touch to a white wicker chair.

OPPOSITE LEFT This haven in light-blue boards was designed by a grandmother to provide a special bed for her grandchild.

OPPOSITE RIGHT Yellow curtains add a splash of cheerful colour to this white-painted child's room.

The bedroom is the oasis of the house. Everything in it should invite relaxation, beginning with the bed. A comfortable country room is not the place for a sharp cosmopolitan design. A bed to establish the mood could be anything from a brass or a painted iron frame to a wooden sleigh bed or a four-poster. But if yours is just a mattress on a bed base, a more mellow look is easily achieved by hanging a quilt, pretty piece of fabric, screen or carved wooden panel behind it to create an informal bedhead.

Soften the bed itself with layers of inviting linen. A tailored cover could look too restrained here. A quilt, a length of charming material or a lace or cotton-crocheted top, turned back to expose sheets and pillows, will look far more appealing. Any old-fashioned bedding will look perfect here: eiderdowns, woollen or cotton blankets folded at the end of the bed or bolsters will all suggest a tempting refuge from the world. Pillows don't have to be slipped into matching covers. A mix of plain cotton with lace-trimmed or embroidered pillowcases is stunning. To finish, pile on cushions in different patterns and fabrics – but in one or two colours only, to keep the look serene.

Bed linen in white looks appealingly pure and fresh, but striped or checked sheets also have the clean, crisp aspect you should strive for. Keep them the same colour in which you have decorated the rest of the room, or the simplicity is lost.

If your ceiling is high, you can have fun above the bed draping canopies in muslin or voile, by threading material through a rounded door knocker, or installing a

OPPOSITE This bedroom is thoroughly stylish yet supremely comfortable. Soothing soft green walls have been dramatically stencilled; vintage bed linen covers the antique iron bed under its striped canopy.

TOP AND ABOVE LEFT Another, more formal canopy, plus sprigged wallpaper and lace at the window, makes a romantic sanctuary. Even the dressing gown hanging on the door has a design contribution to make.

ABOVE RIGHT The unusually patterned and painted iron bed, and the curved arms and legs of the chair, contribute to the great character of this room.

pelmet or tiara-shaped frame against the wall from which to drape fabric. Fix short rails at head height either side of the pillows from which to hang pretty lace panels, and gain privacy and tranquillity.

Beds are conventionally set against a wall, but this needn't be a hard and fast rule. Consider placing the bed lengthwise against a window to catch a view, or against the back of a free-standing cupboard that becomes a screen between the bed and the door.

Somewhere to lay down a book is useful. It doesn't have to be a table; a painted linen chest or a simple wooden chair is an informal touch. A plainly upholstered buttonback chair doubles as a place to read when you don't want to relax on the bed. If there is space a seat – a small sofa at the end of the bed, a

a rug by the bed to land warm toes on each morning is comforting

THIS PAGE AND OPPOSITE In a simple bedroom, the French bed is deliberately set across the window and is dressed almost entirely in blues. Only the bottom sheet, a white embroidered pillowcase glimpsed between a solid and a checked blue pillow, and the blue and white check of the folded blanket provide a break. The room's austerity is toned down by the charming heirloom doll's house set on an old painted box, and the old rag rug by the bed.

modest armchair by a fireplace or window – the room becomes a haven you will enjoy at any time of day, particularly if it contains some of your favourite treasures.

Unless there is a view you would prefer to obscure – in which case a blind in a plain material should do the trick – keep the decoration of your windows as unfussy as you can. Narrow lengths of fabric either side of the window will soften the more metropolitan look of a blind on its own. Curtains should be as plain as possible; one colour in cotton, voile or muslin. If you prefer a patterned fabric, pick a small design. Curtains made from antique sheets or tablecloths can look inspired. Sprigged florals are pretty; checks, stripes and ticking are less feminine alternatives. Hang curtains from a simple wooden or iron pole, with wooden or brass rings, or tabs or ties made from the fabric.

A free-standing armoire or cupboard can convey the kind of informality you are striving for better than built-in cupboards,

OPPOSITE ABOVE RIGHT A carved Asian screen, fixed behind the bed, dominates the room from its central position.

OPPOSITE ABOVE LEFT Here muslin softens strong checks that have been mixed with an Edwardian quilt for striking impact on a white-painted French Directoire bed.

OPPOSITE BELOW Embroidered cushions have a timeless charm.

THIS PAGE An iron bed placed under the eaves and hung with muslins becomes a romantic space and makes full use of a room with a sloping roof, minimizing its awkwardness. The painted dresser echoes the reds in the quilt.

BOTTOM The eye is drawn to this invitingly comfortable armchair by the matching pink frieze that runs round the wall. The reading light confirms that this corner can be used for relaxation at any time.

LEFT Pink is a soothing colour, as these cushions and the soft quilt beneath them demonstrate.

OPPOSITE A bedroom that is merely a place in which to sleep is a waste of valuable space. This should be a room so comfortable and alluring you will be drawn to spending restorative time in it during the day. Here a curvaceous rocking chair and pretty French country chair, in front of an inviting fireplace, encourage the owner to use it as a room in which to sit and read.

although you can soften these with a decorative trim or by cutting shapes in their doors. If a fixed hanging rail is your only option, think about exposing your clothes on wooden hangers or stuffed hangers covered in pretty fabrics, especially if you tend towards clothes in the same colour palette. If you don't think you can keep your clothing tidy enough for public view, run a casual curtain above the rail. The natural texture of hessian or linen scrim looks very effective used in this way. The rail itself could even be made of a length of driftwood.

Strictly speaking, comfortable country bedroom floors should be bare, covered only in rugs. For extra cosseting in the winter months, overlap different rugs all over the floor, editing them back once the weather improves. If you prefer carpet, consider seagrass or sisal or a flat wool weave in a natural tone.

Painted floorboards make a room look bigger and lighter. The colour you choose for your walls will also have an influence: dark shades will not only make the room shrink, but they won't be in keeping with the overall style. Focus on whites – remembering that white itself comes in a range of tones from soft to bright – and pales, or tints of pastels like lavender, fern or rose. Shades of blue give a stronger, more masculine look, if you choose those reflecting the the hues of Provençal pots or warm azures of the Mediterranean.

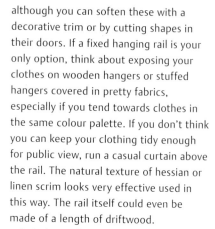

somewhere to sit
makes your bedroom
a restorative
haven

COUNTRY
BATHROOMS

In this room devoted to pampering, gather your favourite things – fine soaps, scents, and sumptuous towels – and relax while you wash away the cares of the day.

in the bathroom
indulge your senses
and promote
well-being

OPPOSITE AND BELOW Victorian flowered tiles make attractive splashbacks. The pretty plates and paintings and mirror were chosen for their Victorian feel.

LEFT A more masculine interpretation of the same look. The mirror above the basin is simply framed, and the English Victorian tiles are restricted to blues.

Having a bath is a superbly comfortable way of slowing down. Bathing is not simply to do with getting clean; a shower can do that. The ritual of running the water, adding a swoosh of scented salts or a glug of luxurious oil, then sliding down for a long soak, makes having a bath a ceremony. Only if your shower is outdoors, and you can scrub under a warm sun or with the twinkle of stars overhead, can the experience of showering be as sensual.

Rolltop or clawfoot baths set in the middle of the room project a restful look, by suggesting there is no need to make

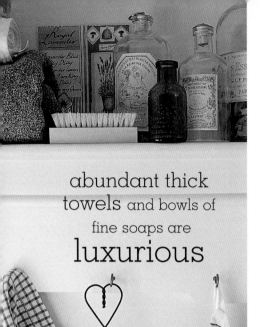

abundant thick
towels and bowls of
fine soaps are
luxurious

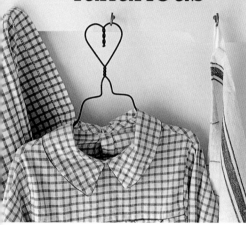

ABOVE This thoughtful display of bathroom equipment is appealing because each article, made from natural materials, is designed without ostentation. There are no garish accessories or oddly fashioned soaps. These glass bottles, printed boxes and cotton towels are plain, yet attractive.

maximum, practical, use of the space. These old-fashioned baths recall the days when a bathroom looked like another sitting room, with a fire in the grate and a sofa or day bed on which to recline. It's an atmosphere you can easily emulate, just by bringing an armchair into the room.

In smaller rooms, set the bath under a window with a pleasant view, or against a wall. A bath on feet – and basin on a pedestal – will make a small room look airier because the eye can travel beyond them to the wall and floor behind. If you want a fixed shower against the wall, pick one with a very large rose for a generous downpour. Hang two shower curtains, pinning each one on alternate curtain rings – something waterproof for inside the rim, with a pretty curtain to disguise it hanging down on the outside.

A wall or sill against which a bath is pushed up will need protection from splashes. A wooden windowsill is a convenient place to keep lotions, but try not to drip over it. Several coats of gloss paint will protect wood. A wall might need a splashback of tiles; several rows of antique tiles produce a country feel.

A narrow bathroom, carved from a convenient corner of the house, can still be a place of comfort. If the bath must be built in, convey a sense of spaciousness by keeping the decoration of the room in one soft shade or white, and add touches of colour through details like towels.

THIS PAGE One of
the critical issues in
bathroom design is
where to store clutter.
Bathrooms are home
to quantities of
bottles, brushes and
bathing equipment,
which if all on view
can make the room
appear chaotic and
an unwelcoming mess.
In this bathroom,
with the handsome
look of its Victorian
mahogany-surround
bath softened by
lace curtains at the
window, all but the
most attractive bottles
are stored away.

If the room is too small for any but a drop-in basin, consider, with the help of a good plumber, installing the basin in the carefully cut out top of an old chest of drawers, rather than having a manufactured bathroom unit. The bowl will take up the first drawer, but the others will provide plenty of room for toiletries, towels or medicines, and the look of the piece will add a comfortable country touch. If there isn't room for such a large item, an antique washstand can be put to work at its original job, housing your bottles and brushes, with towels or magazines stacked on the lower ledge.

Bookshelves are also a storage alternative. Pretty painted ironwork stands with glass shelves look light and airy. Don't limit yourself to filling them with bathing paraphernalia. Why not display some of your favourite china, bowls or jugs? Chairs are useful in bathrooms, to lay clothes or towels upon, as the means

LEFT This bathroom is a simple combination of pale floorboards, ivory-painted tongue-and-groove splashback and a door that draws attention to both the beautiful wood beams around the room and the old cast-iron bath and basin, elegantly painted in rich charcoal. In a clever idea borrowed from the kitchen, hooks run along the towel rail to hold the smaller towels and flannels.

RIGHT A simple wooden chair draws attention to the fact that, while the wooden door has been painted, the plank wall is bare.

of introducing a pattern or colour on a cushion or upholstery, and of course to sit on. You can hang photographs or pictures, as long as the room is well ventilated.

Elsewhere in the house, comfortable country style tends towards simplicity, but in the bathroom luxury and comfort mean abundance. Give in to the desire to pamper yourself by bringing in big natural sponges, wood and natural bristle nailbrushes and backscrubs and old-fashioned china colander soap dishes to hold the current bar of scented soap.

Choose bathmats and towels of a generous size. Stick to a soft palette if you want any colour other than white – pale pinks, blues, greys, taupes or lavender. Striped towels look fresh and pretty, especially when interspersed with others in a single tone. A linen bag dangling behind the door or attractive dressing gowns hung on a row of hooks along a wall are casually decorative possibilities.

Exploit a natural light source with a beautiful panel or curtain of lace, or a length of patterned sheer, to give privacy without blocking the daylight. Good lighting makes a bathroom look bigger and more inviting. Run it off a two-circuit system: lights over mirrors should be strong enough to be useful, and having softer lighting in the ceiling above the bath or around the walls means you can change the mood to fit your own. All you need is time to enjoy it.

ABOVE Pebbles and a toy boat on this bathroom window ledge recall the beach. Bowls of shells or pieces of driftwood used as curtain rails, hooks for robes or sculptural shapes all look pleasing in a bathroom. A tea cloth is an amusing curtain.

OPPOSITE Much is made of the power of reflection here, in the number of mirrors in this tiny space, and in the unusual informal frieze of zinc that runs below the rough shelf. Fragments of mirror and glass pressed into the wall make a light-reflecting mosaic.

COUNTRY
OUTDOORS

An outside space, large or small, offers a sense of renewal. A bench beneath a tree, a row of plants along a windowsill – anything that links us to nature adds an air of ease.

LEFT Don't forget to make time to sit in your glorious garden and savour the results of all your hard work. Choose where and what you sit on carefully so that you make the most of the view. Arbours and bowers create thoroughly romantic settings. Here, prettily sinuous chairs and table are set out for tea under a heady shower of roses.

OPPOSITE TOP A beautifully ornate white-painted wire chair holds its own against an exuberant rose bush, its lines echoing those of the nearby pedestal.

OPPOSITE BELOW LEFT This curved bench is painted in pale grey, a gentler contrast to the vivid dark pink roses arching over it than the more usual white.

OPPOSITE BELOW RIGHT An overhanging canopy of wisteria and a flight of outdoor steps sporting terracotta pots of plants and herbs frame this quiet corner – an ideal shady place to sit.

Eating outdoors, perhaps on a terrace under a vine, conjures up one of the most alluring aspects of comfortable country style. It recalls childhood picnics, romantic dinners under the stars and long lunches with family and friends.

You don't need a vast country garden to achieve the same atmosphere. A small gravelled or paved city patio, terrace or back yard filled with flowering pots can be just as beguiling a venue. Spread a pretty length of fabric or a faded antique cloth over a table, surround it with mismatched chairs and cover it with casual crockery, and you leave the metropolis far behind.

The garden or terrace should be approached as rooms like any other. Decide if you want your outdoor space to be a pretty-parasol, Edwardian-tea-gown place or to have a more market-umbrella, casual-cottons atmosphere. Rattan or woven cane chairs or wooden slatted café chairs with peeling paint look

LEFT A wide stone terrace provides shade from summer heat. Planters and window boxes create a more intimate space on the terrace behind an informal floral barrier.

OPPOSITE A pale pink datura frames a comfortable corner where the flowers inside and out can be enjoyed. A grapevine gives gentle shade. Furniture is kept simple: decoration has been left almost entirely to the plants.

BELOW A cast-iron bench with curving lines fits happily at the entrance to this villa.

wonderfully indolent outside in the sun. Deckchairs with plain cream canvas or sun-bleached Madras stripes are casually comfortable and, along with canvas-seated director's chairs, are easy to fold and store away. Masses of cushions with covers of stripes and florals, tossed onto rugs on the ground or stone benches against a cool wall, make seating especially inviting on drowsy afternoons.

A day bed or steamer chair covered by a full-length cushion in natural textured cotton makes for real elegance outside. Pretty curling ironwork chairs at a small marble-topped table form an inviting spot

ABOVE LEFT The impressive garden room on these pages may be informal, but great care has gone into its decoration. Three enormous architectural windows allow light and air to flood into the room. With its pale butter-coloured walls echoing the sunshine and its high beamed ceiling painted white, the vast space provides a calm and soothing summer sanctuary.

ABOVE RIGHT A bust of Marie Antoinette peeps wittily through the plants. The display can be moved when the room is used for entertaining.

for a morning cup of coffee. Wooden benches, either unpainted, rustic and touched with age and dabs of lichen, or coolly graceful in an undulating shape with a coat of glossy white paint, encourage you to sit and relax at any time of day. Set one under a bower of roses, clematis or wisteria, or between large pots of blooming flowers; once you are seated, there will be little impetus to move.

Unpainted furniture looks more informal than painted, while pieces glossed in white have a fresh appeal that speaks of breezes and boats on sparkling water. Furniture in the vibrant blues, yellows and mellow reds of the Mediterranean will bring a feel of Provence to any setting.

THIS PAGE Stuccoes dot the walls, while plants, pots and stones litter the long table and stand about among watering cans on the pale square-stoned floor, an indication of the casual use to which the room is generally put.

You can define your own comfortable country atmosphere just by laying the table for a meal outside. A blue and white checked cloth, with bowls and plates in robust colours and rustic shapes, establishes quite a different mood from a table laid with delicate, soft-coloured crockery on a pretty damask cloth. The mood will be informal if you forget uniformity and regularity. For a look that is sumptuously generous and casual at the same time, use a plain white sheet as a huge cloth that puddles on the ground. Serving bowls in both vibrant glazes and simple terracotta, one-off pieces that don't match, a harlequin set of glasses, different napkins – a mix of these will combine to create an atmosphere that encourages people to sit back and enjoy themselves.

A weathered picnic table with benches on either side makes an informal setting for lunch outside. With covered pads or a folded quilt to sit on, you add comfort without spoiling the effect. Decorate the table with a terracotta pot of flowers rather than cut blooms and even on a city patio, you make the garden link.

Fill a terrace or a tiny back yard with as many terracotta flower pots in different shapes and sizes as you have room for. Place pots of herbs closest to the table so that diners can reach out to pinch them and release their aromas. Grow highly scented flowers – jasmine, lavender or a rose – by the door into the house to send the smell of sweetness wafting indoors on a breeze.

OPPOSITE A view of the long summer garden seen across the top of the stone table laid for brunch. The different shades of blue around and on this summer table contrast attractively with the bright verdant shade of the blooming garden.

LEFT A bird's eye view of the contrasting patterns of blues. The Mediterranean striped cushions work wonderfully with the tablecloth's checks. Smooth cobblestones form a practical floor beneath the table. Consider where to put a summer table: set on a lawn, the grass will be scuffed before long.

BELOW The porch is a tranquil place for the family to relax.

BOTTOM Summer tables are fun to decorate. The glossy red cherries are echoed in the stems of these wine glasses.

Establish a creeper or vine – easy to grow in most mild climates – and quite soon you will have runners to draw over and create a canopy above your table if you choose. It is a good idea, even in a small space, to make some part of your seating area shaded. A canopy, attached to a wall, which you can reel in and out is one option, a plain umbrella a simpler one. Or keep an umbrella stand full of paper parasols and a basket brimming with sunhats by the garden door.

At night, light candles. You can prevent them from blowing out by putting them inside glass, either shapely hurricane shades or the replacement glass shades sold in department stores for converted Victorian oil lamps. When the night is still, a chandelier filled with candles, hung somewhere the melting wax won't cause problems, makes a stunning effect.

You can create a garden room inside with pots of plants and flowers. Set them on the floor or on a garden bench just inside the door to link with the green outside. Hang a mirror to reflect the garden. Keep everything airy; sit on steamer chairs, cane or willow chairs and floral rugs, and keep any shelving for books or ornaments unobtrusive. Have outdoor things about – a flower-cuttings basket for papers or a farm stool for a side table. Then, when it is too cold to sit in the garden, you will feel refreshed by the sense of almost being in it. Even if an outdoor room means a tiny balcony or a strip of flagstones, make the most of it. Fill it with tubs of flowers and herbs; paint the exterior wall white to increase the light. Pull out the stops for your own comfortable country corner in the sun.

OPPOSITE French doors looking from house to pool make the scene look larger.

BELOW LEFT The French door frames are soft aquamarine, as are the garden chairs. Flower-filled terracotta pots around the base of the walls and along the edge of the terrace add softness and scent to this serene setting.

BELOW RIGHT Under the climbing vine is an outdoor shower. The painted iron armchair dates from the 1930s.

SOURCE DIRECTORY

UNITED KINGDOM
Antiques

THE ANTIQUES
EMPORIUM
The Old Chapel
Long Street, Tetbury
Gloucestershire
GL8 8AA
01666 505281

ANTIQUES & THINGS
77 The Chase
London SW4 0NR
020 7498 1303

HILARY BATSTONE
8 Holbein Place
London SW1W 8NL
020 7730 5335

BAZAR
82 Golborne Road
London W10 5PS
020 8969 6262

DECORATIVE LIVING
55 New King's Road
London SW6 4SE
020 7736 5623

THE DINING
ROOM SHOP
62–64 White Hart
Lane
London SW13 0PZ
020 8878 1020

NICOLE FABRE
592 King's Road
London SW6 2DX
020 7384 3112

GARDINER &
GARDINER
Alfie's Antiques
Market
13–25 Church Street
London NW8 8DT
020 7723 5595

JUDY GREENWOOD
ANTIQUES
657 Fulham Road
London SW6 5PY
020 7736 6037

MARK MAYNARD
ANTIQUES
651 Fulham Road
London SW6 5PU
020 7731 3533

MYRIAD ANTIQUES
131 Portland Road
London W11 4LW
020 7229 1709

PIMPERNEL &
PARTNERS
596 King's Road
London SW6 2DX
020 7731 2448

JOSEPHINE RYAN
ANTIQUES
63 Abbeville Road
London SW4 9JW
020 8675 3900

TOBIAS AND THE
ANGEL
66–68 White Hart
Lane
London SW13 0PZ
020 8878 8902

281 ANTIQUES
281 Lillie Road
London SW6 7LL
020 7385 0706

Decorating

THE BLUE DOOR
74 Church Road
London SW13 0DQ
020 8748 9785

THE CONRAN SHOP
Michelin House
81 Fulham Road
London SW3 6RD
020 7589 7401

CATH KIDSTON
8 Clarendon Cross
London W11 4AP
020 7221 4000

Fabrics

BENNISON FABRICS
16 Holbein Place
London SW1W 8NL
020 7730 8076

CHELSEA TEXTILES
7 Walton Street
London SW3 2JD
020 7584 0111

IAN MANKIN
271 Wandsworth
Bridge Road
London SW6 2TX
020 7371 8825

Flooring

THE CARPET LIBRARY
148 Wandsworth
Bridge Road
London SW6 2UH
020 7736 3664

CRUCIAL TRADING
79 Westbourne
Park Road
London W2 5QH
020 7221 9000

FIRED EARTH
Twyford Mill
Oxford Road
Adderbury
Oxfordshire OX17 3HP
01295 812088
for stockists

SINCLAIR TILL
FLOORING
791–793 Wandsworth
Road
London SW8 3JQ
020 7720 0031

Garden Furniture

CLIFTON LITTLE
VENICE
3 Warwick Place
London W9 2PX
020 7289 7894

JUDY GREEN'S
GARDEN STORE
11 Flask Walk
London NW3 1HJ
020 7435 3832

Kitchen and Tableware

DIVERTIMENTI
139 Fulham Road
London SW3 6SD
020 7581 8065

DAVID MELLOR
4 Sloane Square
London SW1W 8EE
020 7730 4259

SUMMERILL & BISHOP
100 Portland Road
London W11 4LQ
020 7221 4566

Paint

FARROW & BALL
call 01202 876141 for
stockists

FRANCE
Antiques and Decoration

ASTIER DE LA
VILLATTE
5, rue de Médicis
75005 Paris
(0033) 01 43 26 31 25

BETJEMAN ET BARTON
23, boulevard
Malesherbes
75008 Paris
(0033) 01 42 65 86 17

BLANC D'IVOIRE
4, rue Jacob
75007 Paris
(0033) 01 46 33 34 29

LE BON MARCHÉ
24, rue de Sèvres
75007 Paris
(0033) 01 44 39 80 00

CARAVANE
6, rue Pavée
75004 Paris
(0033) 01 44 61 04 20

L'HERBE VERTE
Galérie Vivienne
rue des Petits-Champs
75002 Paris
(0033) 01 40 20 45 09

JOCHEM KLUMPEN
ANTIQUAIRE
'Le quai de la gare'
L'Isle sur Sorgue
Provence
(0033) 04 90 38 57 66

LAPARESSE EN DOUCE
97, rue du Bac
75007 Paris
(0033) 01 42 22 64 10

MAISON DE FAMILLE
10, place de la
Madeleine
75008 Paris
(0033) 01 53 45 82 00

ÉDITH MÉZARD
Château de l'Ange
84220 Lumières
(0033) 04 90 72 36 41

MOKUBA
18, rue Montmartre
75001 Paris
(0033) 01 40 13 81 41

AU NOM DE LA ROSE
46, rue du Bac
75007 Paris
(0033) 01 42 22 22 12

MARIE PAPIER
26, rue Vavin
75006 Paris
(0033) 01 43 26 46 44

LE PASSÉ
D'AUJOURD'HUI
43, rue du Cherche-
Midi
75006 Paris
(0033) 01 42 22 41 21

PORTHAULT
18, avenue Montaigne
75008 Paris
(0033) 01 47 20 75 25

LE PRINCE JARDINIER
Jardins du Palais Royal
75001 Paris
(0033) 01 42 60 37 13

ITALY
Decoration

CRISTINA BELLINI
via San Maurilio, 20
Milano
(0039) 02 89 00 047

BELLORA
via Vincenzo Monti, 27
Milano
(0039) 02 43 90 092

BLANC DE BLANC
corso di Porta
Romana, 6
Milano
(0039) 02 86 66 35

C & C
via della Spiga, 50
Milano
(0039) 02 78 02 57

COMPAGNIA DEI
GIARDINI
via San Maurilio, 4
Milano
(0039) 02 72 02 19 77

LA COMPAGNIA
DELL'ORIENTE
via Santa Marta, 10
Milano
(0039) 02 89 01 30 87

10 CORSO COMO
corso Como, 10
Milano
(0039) 02 29 00 26 74

ECLECTICA
corso Garibaldi, 3
Milano
(0039) 02 87 61 94

MIMMA GINI
via Santa Croce, 21
Milano
(0039) 02 89 40 07 22

PENELOPI 3
via Palermo, 1
Milano
(0039) 02 76 00 06 52

TAGLIETTI E COSTA
via San Marco, 34
Milano
(0039) 02 29 01 12 35

L'UTILE E IL
DILETTEVOLE
via Carlo Maria
Maggi, 6
Milano
(0039) 02 34 53 60 86

PICTURE CREDITS

Key: a=above, b=below, l=left, r=right, c=centre

Page 2 designed by Lorraine Kirke; 3 Melanie Thornton's house in Gloucestershire; 4 refurbishment and interior design by Chichi Meroni Fassio, Parnassus; 5l designer Barbara Davis' own house in upstate New York; 5r Tita Bay's village house in Ramatuelle; 6al Josephine Ryan's house in London; 6ar & br Eleish-van Breems Antiques in Connecticut; 6bl Lincoln Cato's house in Brighton; 7 Maria Vittoria Saibene's country house in Brunello on the lake of Varese; 12 Lee Freund's summerhouse in Southampton, New York; 13 Eva Johnson's house in Suffolk, interiors designed by Eva Johnson; 14 & 15r designed by Lorraine Kirke; 15l Lincoln Cato's house in Brighton; 16l Nelly Guyot's house in Ramatuelle, France, styled by Nelly Guyot; 16r Lincoln Cato's house in Brighton; 17 Eleish-van Breems Antiques in Connecticut; 18–19 designer Barbara Davis' own house in upstate New York; 20 Marisa Cavalli's home in Milan; 21 Josephine Ryan's house in London; 22a Melanie Thornton's house in Gloucestershire; 22bl & 23 Nelly Guyot's house in Ramatuelle, France, styled by Nelly Guyot; 24 designed by Lorraine Kirke; 25 refurbishment

and interior design by Chichi Meroni Fassio, Parnassus; 26l & br Josephine Ryan's house in London; 27 Lee Freund's summerhouse in Southampton, New York; 28 Enrica Stabile's house in Le Thor, Provence; 28 Marisa Cavalli's home in Milan; 30–31 Enrica Stabile's house in Le Thor, Provence; 32 Josephine Ryan's house in London; 34–35 Enrica Stabile's house in Brunello; 36 Enrica Stabile's house in Le Thor, Provence; 38–39 Enrica Stabile's house in Brunello; 40–41 Enrica Stabile's house in Milan; 42–43 designer Barbara Davis' own house in upstate New York; 44 Eva Johnson's house in Suffolk, interiors designed by Eva Johnson; 45l Lincoln Cato's house in Brighton; 46 Marisa Cavalli's home in Milan; 47 Enrica Stabile's house in Milan; 48 & 49a Marisa Cavalli's home in Milan; 49b Eva Johnson's house in Suffolk, interiors designed by Eva Johnson; 50a Eleish-van Breems Antiques in Connecticut; 50bl Enrica Stabile's house in Le Thor, Provence; 51 Nelly Guyot's house in Ramatuelle, France, styled by Nelly Guyot; 52 Ali Sharland's house in Gloucestershire; 53 main Eva Johnson's house in Suffolk, interiors designed by Eva Johnson; 54–55 designer Barbara Davis' own house in upstate New York; 56 Melanie Thornton's house

in Gloucestershire; 57 Tita Bay's village house in Ramatuelle; 58–59 designer Barbara Davis' own house in upstate New York; 60–61 Lincoln Cato's house in Brighton; 62–63 designer Barbara Davis' own house in upstate New York; 64l Melanie Thornton's house in Gloucestershire; 64r Lincoln Cato's house in Brighton; 65 Diana Bauer's house near Cotignac; 66–67 Eva Johnson's house in Suffolk, interiors designed by Eva Johnson; 68–69 Melanie Thornton's house in Gloucestershire; 70 refurbishment and interior design by Chichi Meroni Fassio, Parnassus; 71l Eleish-van Breems Antiques in Connecticut; 71c Ali Sharland's house in Gloucestershire; 72–73 Tita Bay's village house in Ramatuelle; 74 & 75a Nelly Guyot's house in Ramatuelle, France, styled by Nelly Guyot; 75b Diana Bauer's house near Cotignac; 76 designed by Lorraine Kirke; 77 Lee Freund's summerhouse in Southampton, New York; 78 Enrica Stabile's house in Brunello; 79 Ali Sharland's house in Gloucestershire; 80 & 81a Josephine Ryan's house in London; 81b Enrica Stabile's house in Milan; 82l Enrica Stabile's house in Brunello; 82r Maria Vittoria Saibene's country house in Brunello on the lake of Varese; 83 Marisa Cavalli's home in Milan;

84 Ali Sharland's house in Gloucestershire; 86 Lincoln Cato's house in Brighton; 87 Diana Bauer's house near Cotignac; 88 Ali Sharland's house in Gloucestershire; 89 Melanie Thornton's house in Gloucestershire; 90–91 Enrica Stabile's house in Brunello; 92–93 Tita Bay's village house in Ramatuelle; 94–95 refurbishment and interior design by Chichi Meroni Fassio, Parnassus; 96–97 Marisa Cavalli's home in Milan; 98–99 Eva Johnson's house in Suffolk, interiors designed by Eva Johnson; 100 designed by Lorraine Kirke; 101c Ali Sharland's house in Gloucestershire; 102r Enrica Stabile's house in Le Thor, Provence; 103l Marisa Cavalli's home in Milan; 103r Diana Bauer's house near Cotignac; 104 designer Barbara Davis' own house in upstate New York; 105a Enrica Stabile's house in Brunello; 105br Josephine Ryan's house in London; 106–107 designer Barbara Davis' own house in upstate New York; 108al Enrica Stabile's house in Le Thor, Provence; 108r & 109 designed by Lorraine Kirke; 110 Enrica Stabile's house in Brunello; 111 Diana Bauer's house near Cotignac; 112 & 113c designed by Lorraine Kirke; 113l & 114–115 Enrica Stabile's house in Le Thor, Provence; 116 Melanie Thornton's house

in Gloucestershire; 117 designed by Lorraine Kirke; 118–120 Eva Johnson's house in Suffolk, interiors designed by Eva Johnson; 121 designer Barbara Davis' own house in upstate New York; 122 Diana Bauer's house near Cotignac; 123l Enrica Stabile's house in Brunello; 123c Melanie Thornton's house in Gloucestershire; 124 Enrica Stabile's house in Brunello; 125a & bl refurbishment and interior design by Chichi Meroni Fassio, Parnassus; 125br Diana Bauer's house near Cotignac; 126l Enrica Stabile's house in Brunello; 126r refurbishment and interior design by Chichi Meroni Fassio, Parnassus; 127 Eva Johnson's house in Suffolk, interiors designed by Eva Johnson; 128–129 Enrica Stabile's house in Le Thor, Provence; 130 & 131c Nelly Guyot's house in Ramatuelle, France, styled by Nelly Guyot; 131a Lincoln Cato's house in Brighton; 131b designer Barbara Davis' own house in upstate New York; 132 & 133l Enrica Stabile's house in Brunello; 133c designer Barbara Davis' own house in upstate New York; 134–135 Diana Bauer's house near Cotignac; 136 Lee Freund's summerhouse in Southampton, New York; 137 designer Barbara Davis' own house in upstate New York; 141 & 144 designer Barbara Davis' own house in upstate New York.

INTERIOR DESIGNERS WHOSE WORK IS FEATURED IN THIS BOOK

Tita Bay
Interior decorator
via Sudorno, 22D
24100 Bergamo
Italy
t. (0039) 03 52 58 384
Pages 5r, 57, 72–73, 92–93

Lincoln Cato
t. 01273 325334
Pages 6bl, 15l, 16b, 45l, 60–61, 64r, 86, 131a

Marisa Tadiotto Cavalli
via Solferino, 11
20121 Milano
Italy
t. (0039) 02 36 51 14 49
f. (0039) 02 29 00 18 60
mob (0039) 348 41 01 738
marisacavalli@hotmail.com
Pages 20, 28, 46, 48, 49a, 83, 96–97, 102l

Barbara Davis
t. (001) 607 264 3673
Interior design; antique hand-dyed linen, wool, and silk textiles; soft furnishings and clothes to order.
Pages 5l, 18–19, 42–43, 54–55, 58–59, 62–63, 104, 106–107, 120–121, 133c, 141, 144

Eleish-van Breems
Antiques LLC
Thompson House
487 Main Street South
Woodbury
CT 06798, USA
t. (001) 203 263 7030/7031
f. (001) 203 263 7032
evbantiq@wtco.net
www.evbantiques.com
Proprietors: Rhonda Eleish and Edie van Breems
18th- and 19th-century Scandinavian and Northern European antiques, garden elements and decorative accessories, located in the historic Thompson House and garden.
Pages 6ar 6br, 17, 50a, 71l

Nelly Guyot
Interior designer and photographic stylist
12, rue Marthe Edouard
92190 Meudon
France
Pages 16a, 22bl, 23, 51, 74, 75a, 130, 131c

Eva Johnson
Interior designer
t. 01638 731 362
f. 01638 731 855
www.evajohnson.com
Distributor of TRIP-TRAP wood floor treatment products.
Pages 13, 44, 49b, 53l, 66–67, 98–99, 118–119, 127

Kirke Forristal Interior Design
Eclectic, comfortable, unusual proportions with unexpected touches.
18 West 9th Street
New York NY 10011
USA
t. (001) 212 673 3329
f. (001) 212 475 3371
Pages 2, 14, 15r, 24, 76, 100, 108r, 109, 112, 113c, 117

Parnassus
corso Porta Vittoria, 5
Milan
Italy
t. (0039) 02 78 11 07

Pages 4, 25, 70, 94–95, 125a 125 bl, 126r

Sharland & Lewis
52 Long Street
Tetbury
Gloucestershire GL8 8AQ
t. 01666 500354
www.sharlandandlewis.com
Pages 52, 71c, 79, 84, 88, 101c

Enrica Stabile
via Carlo Maria Maggi, 6
20154 Milan
Italy
t. (0039) 02 34 53 60 86
e.stabile@enricastabile.com
www.enricastabile.com
Antiques dealer, interior decorator and photographic stylist.
Pages 28, 30–31, 34–35, 36, 38–39, 40–41, 47, 50bl, 78, 81b, 82l, 90–91, 102 r, 105a, 108al, 110, 113l, 114–115, 123l, 124, 126l, 128–129, 132, 133l

Melanie Thornton
Feels Like Home
t. 07802 286068
Home style consultant.
Pages 3, 22a, 56, 64l, 68–69, 89, 116, 123c

INDEX

Figures in *italics* refer to captions.

ACKNOWLEDGMENTS

Thank you to Gabriella Le Grazie who gave me a second chance after *Open Air Living*
with this wonderful book, so very close to my spirit. Thank you to Julia Watson, who
beautifully expressed through words what I tried to express through pictures.
And a thousand thank yous to Chris Drake who, as always, patient, competent and
dedicated, put up with me and my whimsical character and with unflagging good humour
again produced superb photographs. Thank you to all the fantastic people who very
generously shared their houses with us: Diane Bauer, Tita Bay, Jill and Lincoln Cato,
Marisa Cavalli, Barbara Davis, Nelly Guyot, Rhonda Eleish, Eva Johnson, Lorraine Kirke,
Giulana & Federico Magnifico, Maria Cristina Meroni Fassio, Lee Freund, Josephine Ryan,
Toia Saibene, Ali Sharland, Melanie Thornton, Elisabeth van Breems. Thank you to Alberto
Bellinzona, a hardworking, creative, resourceful and very capable assistant.
Thank you to Clare Double, to Vicky Holmes and the team at RPS who smoothed,
rushed...and eventually produced *Comfortable Country*.